SRA
Open Court
Reading

Meg's Sled

A Division of The **McGraw·Hill** Companies

Columbus, Ohio

SRA/McGraw-Hill

A Division of The **McGraw·Hill** Companies

Copyright © 2000 by SRA/McGraw-Hill.

Printed in the United States of America.

Send all inquiries to:
SRA/McGraw-Hill
8787 Orion Place
Columbus, OH 43240-4027

ISBN 0-02-660849-9
3 4 5 6 7 8 9 PBM 04 03 02 01 00

Meg pulled a sled up the hill.
Meg passed Helen Hen.
"Help me pull this sled," called Meg.
"I can't," said Helen Hen.

3

Meg pulled and pulled.
Meg passed Bob Bobcat.
"Help me pull this sled," called Meg.
"I can't," said Bob Bobcat.

Meg pulled and pulled.
She passed Bill Bulldog.
"Help me pull this sled," called Meg.
"I can't," said Bill Bulldog.

Meg got to hill's top.
Meg unpacked the sled and got on.

Meg sped past Bill Bulldog.
Meg sped past Bob Bobcat.
Meg sped past Helen Hen.

Meg and the sled sped on until seven.